MASKS
OF THE WORLD
Coloring Book

A. G. Smith

DOVER PUBLICATIONS, INC.
Mineola, New York

Publisher's Note

Down through the ages, masks have served many functions: as protection or disguise, as a part of dances and ritual, to represent gods and demons, in battle to frighten the enemy, by hunters stalking their prey, and in numerous other areas of human life. Ranging from tiny amulets to huge totem poles, masks can be made of wood, metal, shell, fiber, horn, stone, leather, paper, cloth–almost any material. This book contains a rich cross-section of thirty masks from around the world and across the ages, including a mask representing the ancient Egyptian god Bes, an Italian Renaissance mask of a faun, and a twentieth–century Chinese New Year's mask. As you color these accurate depictions, you'll develop an increased appreciation of the importance and universality of masks and their varied roles in cultures across the globe.

Bibliographical Note

Masks of the World Coloring Book is a new work, first published by Dover Publications, Inc., in 2003.

DOVER *Pictorial Archive* SERIES

International Standard Book Number: 0-486-43039-1

Manufactured in the United States of America
Dover Publications, Inc., 31 East 2nd Street, Mineola, N.Y. 11501

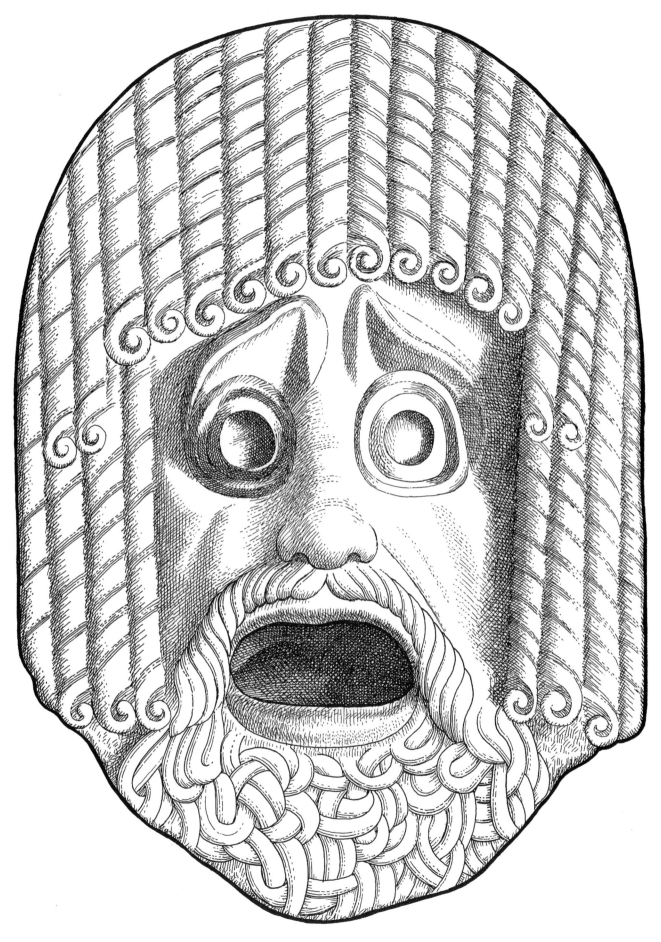

1. Early Rome–Tragic Mask

2. Ancient Roman Gorgon Mask

3. Italian Renaissance–Mask of Faun

4. North America–Kwakiutl Transformation Mask

5. Alaskan Inuit Mask

6. Mexican Death Mask

7. Hopi Kachina Mask

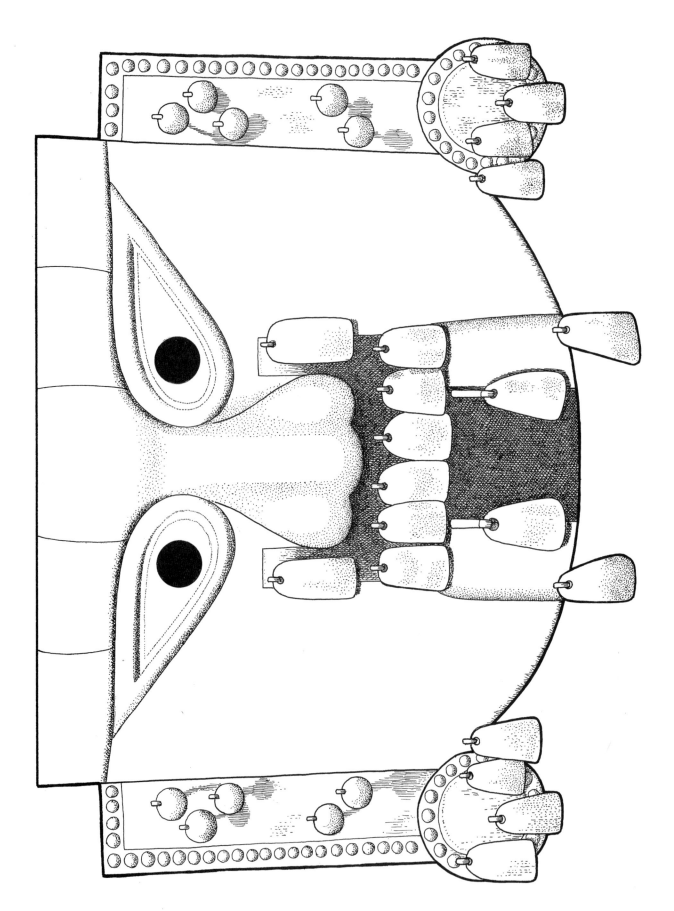

8. Peru–Chima Mask, painted gold, ca. 1200 A.D.

9. **Guatemala–Maya Jade Mask (8th century)**

10. Africa–Bakuba Dance Mask

11. Mask of Egyptian God Bes

12. Cameroon–Wooden Animal Mask

13. West Africa–Woman's Ceremonial Mask

14. Nigeria–Hippopotamus Water Spirit Mask

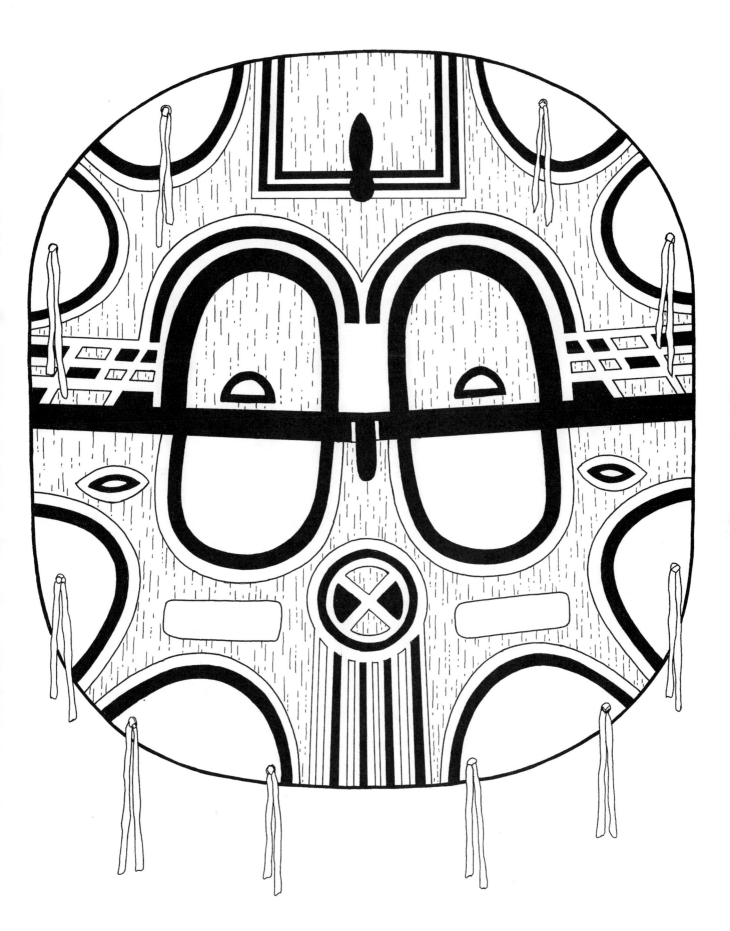

15. Congo–Bateke Mask

16. Borneo–Dance Mask

17. New Ireland (New Guinea region) Dance Mask

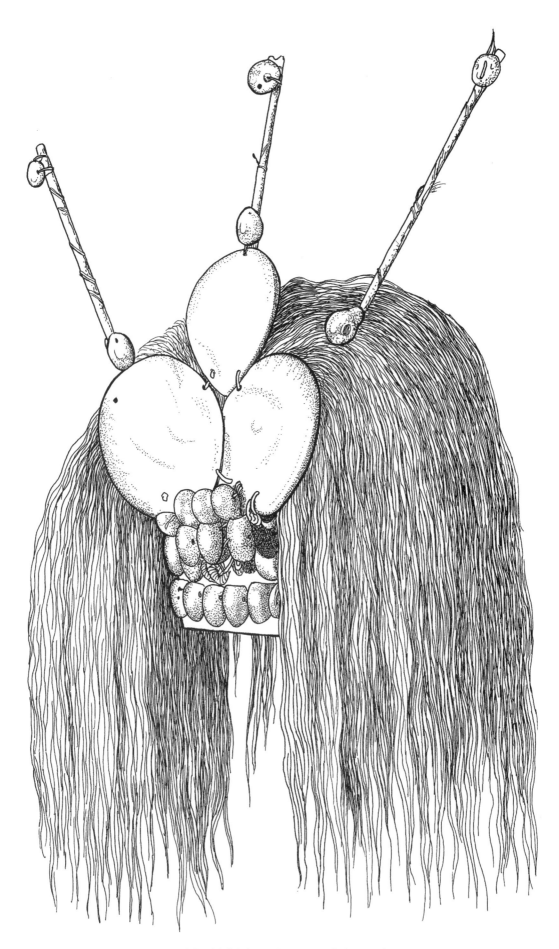

18. Tahitian Ceremonial Mask

19. New Caledonia (Oceania) Water Spirit Mask

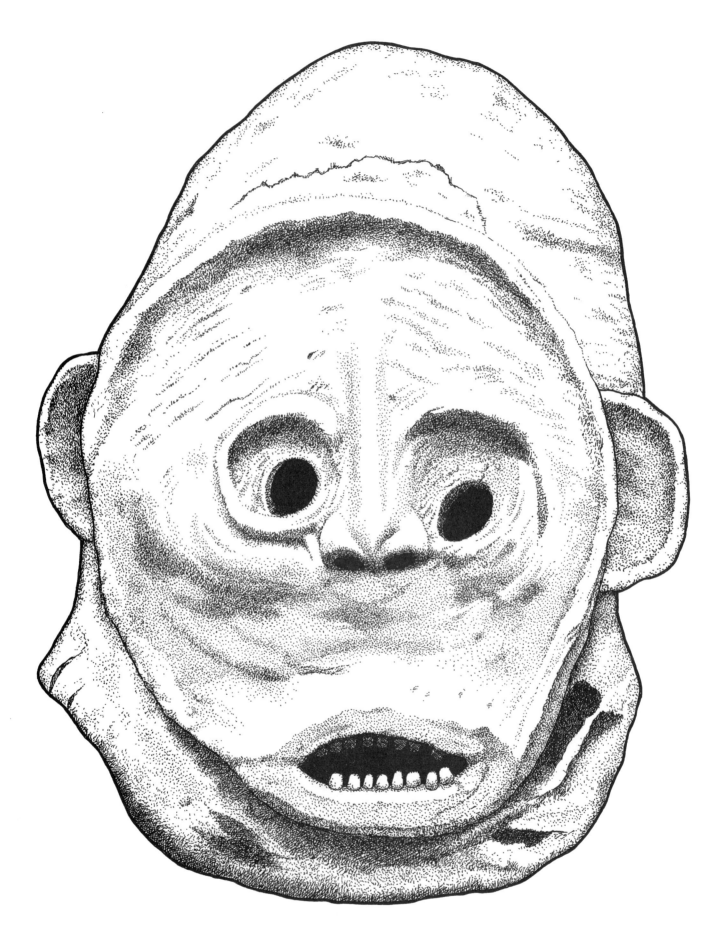

20. New Guinea–Asaro "Mud Man" Mask

21. New Hebrides (Oceania) Ritual Mask

22. India–Narasimha Mask

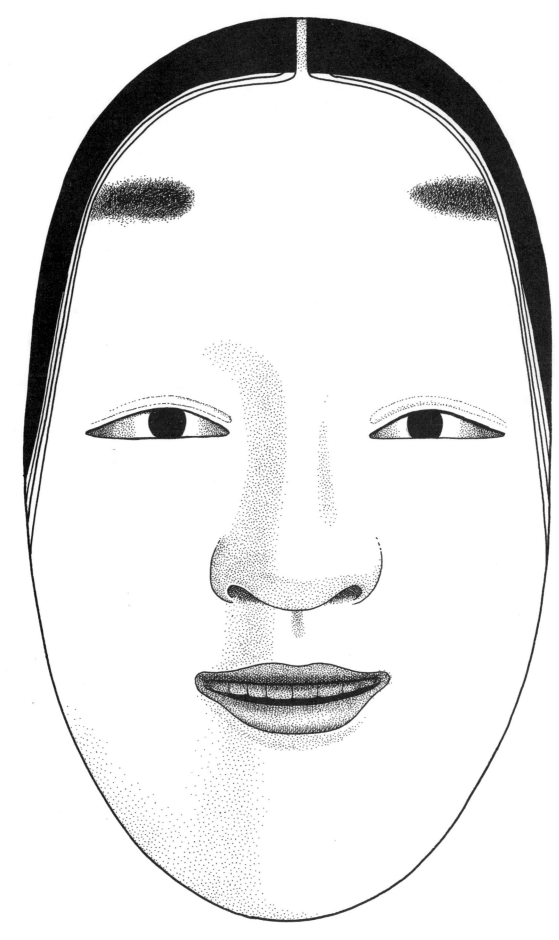

23. Japan–No Theater Mask for Young Woman

24. Japan–Funerary Mask (13th – 14th century)

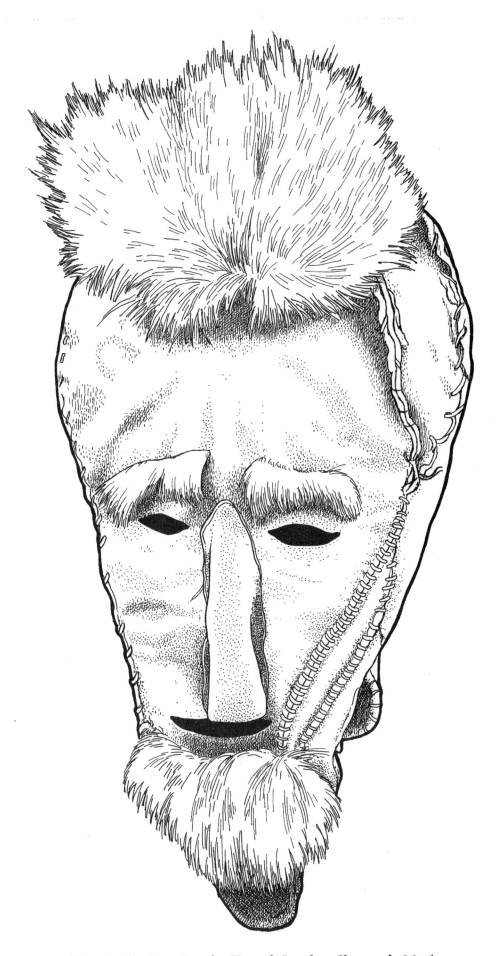

25. Far Eastern Russia–Koryak Leather Shaman's Mask

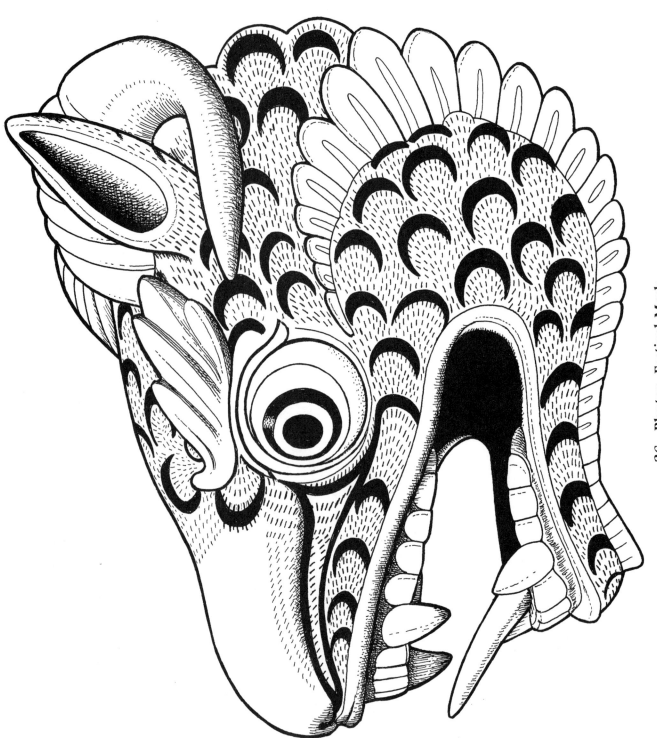

26. Bhutan–Festival Mask

27. Burma (Myanmar)–Papier-Mâché Mask of Tiger

28. Sri Lanka–Cobra Mask

29. Chinese Theater Mask

30. China–Lion Mask for New Year's Festival (20th century)